Headlines

General Editor: John L. Foster

Exploring Space
John L. Foster

Edward Arnold

© John L. Foster 1979

First published 1979 by
Edward Arnold (Publishers) Ltd
41 Bedford Square
London WC1B 3DQ

All Rights Reserved. No part of this publication may be reproduced, stored in a retrieval system, or transmitted in any form or by any means, electronic, mechanical, photocopying, recording or otherwise, without the prior permission of Edward Arnold (Publishers) Ltd.

For Ian and Simon who helped a lot

British Library Cataloguing in Publication Data

Foster, John Louis
   Exploring space.—(Headlines; 12).
   1. Readers—1950–
   I. Title   II. Series
   428'.6'2   PE1121

ISBN 0–7131–0342–6

Acknowledgements
Associated Press: 6, 11, 15; Keystone Press Agency: 14, 19, 33, 42, 43, 44, 47; Nasa: cover, 23, 25, 32, 35, 38, 41, 46; Novosti Press Agency: 5, 40; Popperfoto: 29; Tass: 28; United Press International: 8.

Text set in 12/14 pt Photon Baskerville, printed by photolithography, and bound in Great Britain at The Pitman Press, Bath

Contents

The First Spaceflights	4
The Race to the Moon	13
Exploring the Moon	24
Towards the Planets and Beyond	36

The First Spaceflights

It was just before eleven o'clock in the morning on 12 April 1961. A young girl and her grandmother were standing outside their home near a small Russian village. Suddenly the girl looked up and pointed. 'Look Grandma,' she said, 'something's falling out of the sky.'

The girl and her grandmother watched the strange object as it fell towards the Earth. They wondered what it could be. They did not realise that they were watching the final moments of man's first-ever spaceflight.

The World's First Spaceman

The spacecraft was called Vostok 1. It had been launched one hour forty-eight minutes earlier. It was a small sphere about 2.3 metres in diameter with 3 portholes and 3 entry hatches. Inside was a 27-year-old Russian Air Force officer called Yuri Gagarin.

At its highest point Vostok 1 reached about 327 kilometres above the Earth. It made one orbit and then parachuted safely back to Earth. Yuri Gagarin had become the world's first spaceman.

The Vostok spacecraft after landing

The First Satellite

Three and a half years earlier on 4 October 1957 the Russians had launched the first man-made object into space. The first satellite was called Sputnik 1 and was a sphere of about 58 centimetres in diameter. It weighed 83.6 kilograms – about the weight of a large man.

It carried two radios and was fitted with 4 whip-type aerials. It broadcast signals to Earth for 21 days until its batteries ran down. Then it continued to orbit the Earth for another 75 days before it broke up.

The successful launching of Sputnik 1 was a triumph for Russia's scientists. The United States had hoped to be the first country to send up a satellite.

But the Vanguard rocket programme had run into difficulties. It was not until 31 January 1958 that the first American satellite, Explorer 1, was successfully launched. The race began to see which country could become the first to put a man into space.

Laika

Already the Russians had sent a living creature into space. When Sputnik 2 was launched on 3 November 1957 it carried a passenger, a dog called Laika. The purpose of Laika's flight was to see how she was affected by being weightless. Because there is no gravity, when a man travelled in space he would become weightless. No one was sure what effects being weightless might have.

For 7 days Sputnik 2 sent back radio signals giving information about Laika. Then her oxygen

Laika in Sputnik 2

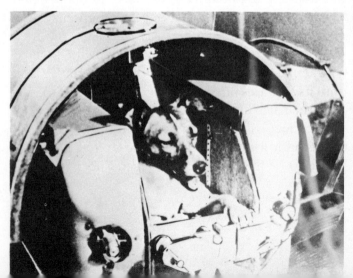

supply ran out and she died painlessly. Laika was the first living creature to travel in space. Her journey showed that manned spaceflight might be possible. But first the scientists would have to solve the problem of how to bring a spacecraft safely back to Earth.

Belka and Strelka

It was two and a half years before the Russians were ready to try to bring a spacecraft back from space. The first attempt was a failure. But three months later, in August 1960, Sputnik 5 was launched. It carried two dogs – Belka and Strelka. They completed 18 orbits before re-entry was attempted. All went according to plan. Once inside the Earth's atmosphere the dogs were ejected from the spacecraft and parachuted safely down to Earth.

Setbacks

However, in December 1960 the Russian space programme suffered a setback. Sputnik 6 was launched, and the attempt to recover it failed. Its dog passenger was killed.

The Americans were also having their problems. The first American space traveller was a monkey called Miss Sam. Now, on 31 January 1961, Mercury 2 was launched. Its passenger was Ham, a chimpanzee.

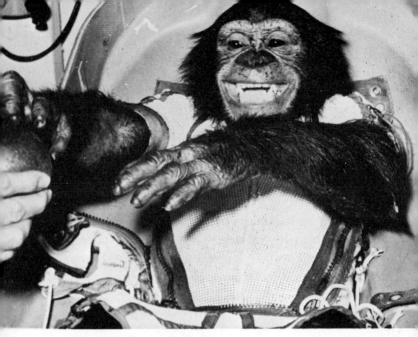

Ham stretches out for the apple with a huge grin

An Eventful Journey

Ham's journey was an eventful one. The spacecraft travelled over 2000 k.p.h. faster than planned and reached a height of 253 kilometres instead of 185 kilometres. It landed over 200 kilometres from its target and was beginning to sink by the time the recovery helicopters reached it. But Ham had worked throughout the flight and was none the worse for his adventure. When the capsule was opened he was offered an apple. He took it with a huge grin!

The Americans were encouraged by Ham's safe

return. They were not yet ready to send a manned spacecraft to orbit the Earth, but soon they might be able to send a man into space. They might still beat the Russians. They hurried to prepare the next Mercury flight.

While they were doing so, in March 1961 the Russians launched two more Sputniks. Both of them carried dogs and both were successfully recovered. Everything was now ready for Gagarin's historic flight. On 12 April 1961 Russia became the first country to send a man into space.

Undamaged

Less than a month later, on 5 May 1961, the American Alan Shepherd, in Mercury 3, became the world's second spaceman. All went according to plan and the spacecraft returned to Earth undamaged. Shepherd's flight lasted only 15 minutes 22 seconds. But less than 10 years afterwards he spent 9 days in space as commander of Apollo 14. As well as being the second man into space Alan Shepherd became only the fifth man to walk on the moon.

'A Bit Scared'

Shepherd's flight had gone so well that in July 1961 the Americans sent up their second astronaut – Gus Grissom. Before the flight he admitted that he was 'a bit scared'. The flight itself went smoothly and the capsule splashed down as planned. But, while Grissom was waiting for the rescue helicopter, the hatch-cover blew off. The capsule started to sink. Grissom had to climb out and hurriedly swim away. He was hauled safely aboard the helicopter, but the capsule sank and was never recovered.

Russia Leads the Way

In February 1962 John Glenn became the first American astronaut to orbit the Earth, ten months after Gagarin had done so. Already the Russian Herman Titov had spent a whole day in space. The Americans struggled to catch up with the Russians. But during the early years of manned space flight it was the Russians who led the race into space.

In August 1962 Russia became the first country to send two manned spacecraft into orbit at the same time. Vostok 4 was launched a day after Vostok 3 and they passed within 5 kilometres of each other.

The World's First Spacewoman

Another joint flight took place in June 1963. Vostok 5 set up a space record of nearly 5 days and 81 orbits, which lasted for more than 2 years. Its partner Vostok 6 also made history, for the pilot was 26-year-old Valentina Tereschkova – the world's first spacewoman. She spent 70 hours 50 minutes in space and completed 48 orbits before returning safely to Earth.

Valentina Tereschkova, the world's first spacewoman, samples food from a tube

Five months after the flight Valentina Tereschkova married another cosmonaut, Andrian Nikolayev, who had been the pilot of Vostok 3. A year later their daughter was born – the first child whose parents had both travelled in space!

The First Spacewalk

As early as October 1964 the Russians sent up the first 3-man spacecraft – Voskhod 1. Then, in March 1965, Alexei Leonov, one of the two cosmonauts in

Voskhod 2, made the first spacewalk. He spent ten minutes floating freely in space, joined to the capsule by a short cable. He flew no less than 5000 kilometres at a speed of 29 000 k.p.h.! He could travel at such a speed because there is no air in space to cause friction. Nearer to Earth, both he and the spacecraft would have burned up.

Afterwards Leonov described what it felt like to swim through space. 'I would give a little pull on the line', he said, 'and it would send me moving towards the hull. Then I would push off again and be carried outwards spinning slightly. The scene in front of my eyes was fantastic: first the stars in all their glory sewn into a ground of black velvet, then the surface of the Earth . . . It was like floating over a huge, colourful map, more wonderful than any painting.'

A Major Crisis

After Leonov had returned to the capsule a major crisis occurred. The automatic re-entry system failed. For the first time a Russian cosmonaut had to fire the retro-rocket himself. However, all went well. Voskhod 2 landed safely in deep snow about 2000 kilometres north of its target. The cosmonauts had to wait two and a half hours for the first rescue helicopter. But they were both unhurt and Leonov was unharmed by his walk in space.

The Race to the Moon

Five days after Leonov made his walk in space the Americans launched their first two-man capsule – Gemini 3. Its pilots were Gus Grissom and John Young and it was the first spacecraft to carry a computer into space.

During 1965 and 1966 no less than 10 Gemini spacecraft were launched. The aim of the Gemini programme was to provide America's scientists with enough knowledge about space travel to be able to put a man on the moon.

The Longest Manned Spaceflight

In December 1965 Frank Borman and Jim Lovell in Gemini 7 set a new record for the longest manned spaceflight. They spent 14 days in space. They flew round the Earth 206 times and covered 9.2 million kilometres – 23 times the distance between the Earth and the Moon. When they stepped aboard the recovery ship they walked a little unsteadily, but otherwise they were fit and well.

During Gemini 7's record-breaking flight, Gemini 6 made a one-day flight. It was able to fly right up to Gemini 7 and at one point was only 1.83 metres away. Then, in March 1966, Neil Armstrong

Gemini 6 and 7—just over a metre apart!

and David Scott carried out the first space docking by linking their Gemini 8 spacecraft to a target rocket.

Out of Control

But soon after the docking there was a crisis. The two vehicles started to tumble and spin. One of the thrusters had jammed. The spacecraft was out of control.

It was America's first space emergency. The astronauts had to fire the retro-rockets. They managed to bring the spacecraft back under control, but had to return to Earth two days early.

Unmanned Spacecraft

Throughout the 1960s Russia's space programme, like America's, was centred on the Moon. The Russians had beaten the Americans into space, but would they be able to win the race to the moon?

As early as 1959 the Russians had sent an unmanned spacecraft to the Moon. Luna 2, launched on 12 September 1959, had crashed on the Moon carrying the Russian flag. Less than a month later Luna 3 had passed behind the Moon and sent back the first pictures of the far side, which cannot be seen from Earth.

The First Soft-Landing

Five more Luna spacecraft had been launched between 1963 and 1965. The aim was to make a soft-landing on the Moon. But two of the spacecraft missed the Moon and the other three crashed. It was February 1966 before Luna 9 made the first successful soft-landing. It was built so that it would

One of the first ever close-up photographs of the Moon taken from Luna 9

roll into an upright position when it landed, and for three days it sent back pictures of the Moon's landscape. Then, in March 1966, Luna 10 became the first spacecraft to orbit the Moon.

The Americans also sent up unmanned spacecraft to obtain information about the Moon. Already three Ranger spacecraft had taken 17 000 close-up photographs of the Moon's surface. Now 5 Lunar Orbiter spacecraft sent back pictures, and carried out tests, while orbiting the Moon. Then in April 1967 Surveyor 3 made a soft-landing and used a scoop to dig a trench in the Moon's surface.

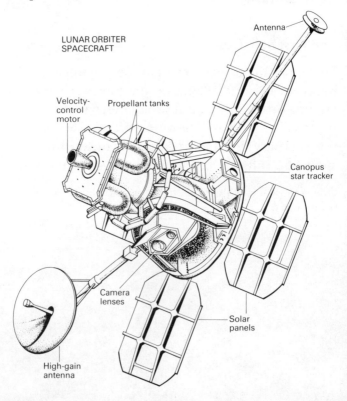

Disaster

By 1967 both America and Russia were ready to test the new spacecraft they had been developing for manned flight. But the tests ended in disaster.

On 27 January 1967 the American astronauts Gus Grissom, Edward White and Roger Chaffee climbed aboard an Apollo spacecraft on the launching-pad. The Saturn rocket beneath the 3-man capsule was empty, but otherwise everything was working as if it was a real take-off. The astronauts were wearing their spacesuits, the hatch was sealed and the countdown was taking place.

Fire in the Capsule!

Suddenly there was a shout: 'Fire! Fire in the capsule!' Before anyone could do anything, it was too late. The three astronauts were dead.

A long enquiry was held. It was found that there had been a fault in the wiring system. Several changes had to be made in the spacecraft and the first manned Apollo flight did not take place until 18 months later.

Another Tragedy

There was another tragedy in April 1967 when the Russians launched the first of their new spacecraft, Soyuz 1. There appear to have been some flight problems and re-entry was ordered after only 18 orbits. At a height of 7000 metres the lines of the main parachute became twisted. The capsule crashed to the ground. The pilot, Vladimir Komarov, was killed.

The next manned spaceflight did not take place until October 1968. Meanwhile, unmanned spacecraft continued to gather information about the Moon.

Zond 5

In September 1968 the Russians appeared to have taken the lead in the space race. The Russian unmanned Zond 5 became the first spacecraft to travel round the Moon and return safely to Earth. It carried tortoises, insects and seeds, none of which were harmed in any way by their journey.

Man's First Journey Round the Moon

Now, however, the Americans were ready to send the first of their Apollo spacecraft to the Moon. Early in the morning on 21 December 1968 Apollo 8 was launched from Cape Kennedy. Astronauts Frank Borman, James Lovell and William Anders set off on man's first journey round the Moon.

The first part of the journey went smoothly and on Christmas Eve Apollo 8 approached the Moon. At Mission Control everyone waited anxiously as Apollo 8 passed behind the Moon. When a

Apollo 8 leaves the launching pad at Cape Kennedy

spacecraft goes behind the Moon it loses radio contact with Earth. While Apollo 8 was behind the Moon the astronauts had to fire the braking rocket to put the spacecraft into orbit round the Moon. If anything went wrong, there was nothing Mission Control could do to help them.

No Problems

But there were no problems. The firing was successful. For 20 hours Apollo 8 orbited the Moon, and sent back TV pictures to viewers on Earth. The astronauts studied the Moon's surface and took pictures of possible landing sites. 'The colour of the soil', said William Anders, 'is a very whitish grey – like a dirty beach with millions of footprints on it.'

On Boxing Day 1968 the first men to travel round the Moon returned to Earth after a journey of nearly a million kilometres. They splashed down in the Pacific Ocean only 11 seconds earlier than planned!

A Triumph

Apollo 8's flight was a triumph for America's scientists. Now they were almost certainly ahead of the Russians. They felt sure that they could win the race to the Moon.

Two more Apollo test flights were held early in 1969. Both were successful and on 16 July 1969

Apollo 11 stood on the launching-pad at Cape Kennedy. The Americans were ready to attempt the first manned landing on the Moon.

'The Eagle has Landed'

The flight to the Moon was uneventful and 4 days after lift-off Apollo 11 began to orbit the Moon. The following day two of the astronauts – Neil Armstrong and Edwin Aldrin – entered the LEM, or lunar excursion module, which had been codenamed Eagle. The lunar module would land

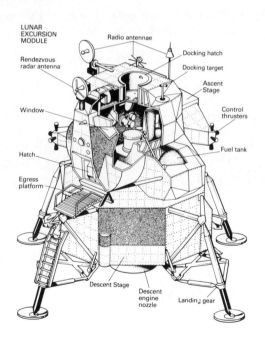

them on the Moon. Then, when they were ready, its upper half would take them back to the main capsule or command module. While they were on the Moon the third astronaut, Michael Collins, would orbit the Moon in the command module, waiting to pick them up for the return journey to Earth.

After checking their instruments Armstrong and Aldrin were ready to make the landing. On Earth it was 9 o'clock in the evening on Sunday 20 July 1969. Millions of people gathered round their radio and TV sets to listen. The journey in Eagle took 12 minutes. As they neared the landing site Armstrong saw that it was covered with boulders. He steered the spacecraft further to the west. Then, to everyone's relief, he announced: 'The Eagle has landed.'

The First Men on the Moon

Six and three-quarter hours later at 3.56 a.m. on Monday 21 July Neil Armstrong crawled backwards out of the hatch of the lunar module. He put his feet on the small platform outside and began to climb down the ladder attached to the landing leg. As he put his left foot on the Moon's surface he said, 'That's one small step for a man; one giant leap for mankind.'

Just over a quarter of an hour later Edwin Aldrin joined him on the surface of the Moon. Together they put up a 1.52 metre United States flag. The Americans had won the race to put men on the Moon!

Astronaut Edwin Aldrin steps down from the lunar module

Exploring the Moon

Armstrong and Aldrin spent two and a quarter hours on the Moon. They collected 20 kilograms of moonrock and moondust to bring back to Earth for scientists to study, and set up several scientific experiments. They had a telephone call from the President of the United States, and uncovered a message which had been fixed to the spacecraft's ladder. It said: 'Here men from the Planet Earth first set foot upon the Moon, July 1969 A.D. We came in peace for all mankind.'

Like a Pair of Kangaroos

People on Earth watched on TV as Armstrong and Aldrin hopped about in the moondust like a pair of kangaroos. On the Moon everything weighs six times less than it does on Earth, because the Moon has less gravity. But the astronauts have to wear bulky spacesuits. Besides, they are so used to walking on the Earth that they find it hard to get used to weighing so much less.

A Close Check

The journey back to Earth was uneventful. Apollo 11

Edwin Aldrin on the Moon photographed by Neil Armstrong, commander of Apollo 11. The lunar module next to Aldrin can be seen reflected in his vizor.

splashed down in the Pacific on 24 July 1969 only 30 seconds later than planned. The three astronauts changed into special clothes. For the next three weeks they lived together, without coming into direct contact with other human beings.

Doctors kept a close check on them. They had to be sure the astronauts had not picked up any germs while they were on the Moon. The three weeks passed without the astronauts showing signs of any strange diseases. They were given the all clear.

Struck by Lightning

Plans were made for further trips to the Moon and in November 1969 Apollo 12 was launched. The lift-off took place in bad weather. Immediately afterwards the rocket was struck by lightning. Mission Control lost radio contact and the spacecraft's electrical system was put out of action for a short time.

It looked as if the moon trip would have to be called off. While the spacecraft orbited the Earth a complete check was carried out. Everything was still in working order. Mission Control gave the go-ahead for the flight to continue.

On Target

Again the moonlanding was successful. The lunar module touched down exactly on target – only 183 metres away from the Surveyor 3 spacecraft, which had soft-landed in the Ocean of Storms two and a half years earlier. On one of the two moonwalks Charles Conrad became the first man to fall on the Moon. But Alan Bean quickly helped him to his feet and he was unhurt. The only thing that really went wrong on the mission was that the lunar module's TV camera was burnt out when Bean accidentally pointed it at the sun.

Unlucky Thirteen

The next moonflight almost ended in disaster. Some people think that thirteen is an unlucky number. It certainly was for astronauts Jim Lovell, Fred Haise and John Swigert. Their spacecraft was Apollo 13. It lifted off at 13.13 hours on 11 April 1969. Then, two days later, on 13 April an explosion occurred that damaged the spacecraft so badly that the moonlanding had to be called off.

The damage was so serious that the astronauts had to move into the lunar module and use it as a lifeboat. It was touch and go whether Mission Control would be able to bring them back to Earth safely. As the crippled spacecraft headed back towards Earth everyone kept their fingers crossed. Had the explosion damaged the heat-shield? Would the spacecraft burn up when it re-entered the Earth's atmosphere?

'A Triumphant Failure'

When re-entry takes place Mission Control loses contact with the spacecraft for a short time. All over the world people watching their TV sets held their breath. Suddenly there was a voice on the radio and there was the spacecraft. It was all over. The first space rescue had been made. Instead of a disaster Apollo 13's flight became 'a triumphant failure'.

Ten months later in February 1971 Apollo 14 made the third successful moonlanding. The astronauts on the first three Apollo moonlandings were only able to explore the area within walking distance of the lunar module. Plans were now made to send up a moon motor car.

From the film *Trip to the Sea of Rains* Luna 17 lands on the Moon.

A model of the first lunar robot—Lunokhod 1

A Desperate Attempt

Already the Russians had used a robot motor vehicle to explore part of the Moon's surface. In 1969, just before Armstrong and Aldrin's triumphant return in Apollo 11, the Russians had made a desperate attempt to land an unmanned spacecraft to collect some moondust. But Luna 15 had crashed. It was September 1970 before Luna 16 became the first unmanned spacecraft to land on the Moon and return to Earth carrying moondust.

The First Moon Robot

In November 1970 Luna 17 had been launched. It carried the first moon robot – Lunokhod 1. Luna 17 made a soft-landing on the flat plain called the Sea of Rains. Scientists in Russia's Deep Space Communications Centre used TV cameras on the spacecraft to check that no boulders were in the way. Then a ramp was lowered and Lunokhod 1 rolled down onto the Moon's surface.

It had been expected to work for 90 days. In fact it worked for 11 months and was one of Russia's greatest space successes. During that time it travelled over 10 500 metres, sent back 20 000 separate photographs and studied the Moon's soil in 500 different places.

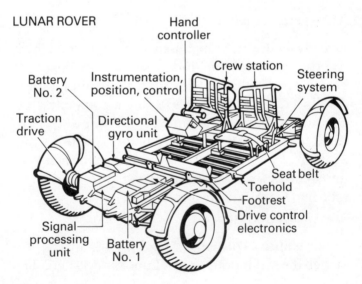

LUNAR ROVER

The Lunar Rover

The moon car which the Americans built was called the lunar rover. It looked rather like an open jeep. It had a battery-driven electric motor and could reach a speed of 16.9 k.p.h. It weighed only 209 kilograms and folded up like a sun bed so that it could be stored easily during the flight.

The first spacecraft to carry a lunar rover was Apollo 15. Before it was launched the launchpad was struck by lightning no less than 11 times! But the countdown went smoothly and the lift-off took place only 0.008 seconds late.

'Like a Real Bucking Bronco'

The mission was a huge success and the astronauts brought back a vast amount of scientific information. At first they had problems with the lunar rover's steering. But otherwise they were delighted with it, even though it bounced them along 'like a real bucking bronco.'

Anxious Moments

There was an anxious moment as Apollo 15 returned to Earth. For the first time during re-entry one of the spacecraft's three 25.3 metre parachutes failed to open. However, they splashed down safely and neither the spacecraft nor the crew were harmed.

There were anxious moments too during Apollo

16's flight. At one stage, just before the moonlanding, it looked as though the landing might have to be called off. But the problem was solved and the landing was able to go ahead, even though it took place 6 hours later then planned.

Grand Prix Trials

Once again a lunar rover was used and astronauts John Young and Charles Duke drove 27 kilometres in it. A highlight of the mission came at the end of one of their journeys when Young carried out some 'Grand Prix' trials. He drove the lunar rover flat out in circles and skidded it round in order to test the wheel grip.

Grand Prix trials on the moon!

The last of the Apollo moon missions this century: Schmitt examines a huge lunar boulder

A Record Load

During the final moonlanding from Apollo 17 in December 1972 astronauts Gene Cernan and Jack Schmitt spent 22 hours 6 minutes outside the lunar module. They travelled 35 kilometres in the lunar rover and collected a record load of 113 kilograms of moon rocks.

There had been a tense and exciting start to the

mission. It was the first time that the launch took place at night. The countdown was under way. It was now only 30 seconds to lift off. Suddenly the countdown stopped. There were problems with one of the rocket's fuel tanks.

The countdown clocks were put back to 22 minutes before take-off while the fault was traced. They were started again, but with 8 minutes to go there was another hold up. Finally, Apollo 17 lifted off two hours forty minutes late.

False Alarms

During the journey to the Moon a series of master alarms went off. But they were all false alarms. Then on the journey home the astronauts lost a pair of scissors. Everyone was worried, because one of the astronauts could easily have been killed by them flying around during re-entry. The astronauts searched everywhere, but they were never found. They must have drifted off into space, while one of them was making a spacewalk.

The last Apollo mission ended safely when Apollo 17 splashed down in the Pacific only 6.4 kilometres from the recovery ship. The Apollo Project had been a triumph for America's scientists. Man had taken his first major step in the exploration of space.

Apollo 17 lift-off

Towards the Planets and Beyond

Men can fly to the Moon in three days. Spaceflights to other planets take months or even years. Already plans are being made for manned spaceflights to Mars. The journey there and back would last 590 days and would cost at least 40 000 million dollars. But many problems still have to be solved before man can set out on his first journey to another planet.

First Pictures of Another Planet

During the 1960s both America and Russia began to prepare for journeys to the planets by sending unmanned spacecraft to Venus and Mars. In 1962 America's Mariner 2 became the first spacecraft to fly past Venus and send back information about it. Two and a half years later, during July 1965, Mariner 4 passed within 10 000 kilometres of Mars and sent back to Earth the first close-range pictures of another planet.

Less than 100 years ago many people believed that intelligent life might exist on Mars. They thought that the lines running across the red Martian deserts might be canals and that the dark areas were patches of vegetation. What would the photographs tell us about the red planet?

In Orbit Round Mars

The first pictures showed that Mars was covered in craters and that the dark areas were not patches of vegetation. In 1969 two further Mariner spacecraft sent back more pictures; then in November 1971 Mariner 9 became the first spacecraft to go into orbit round Mars. It sent back over 7000 TV pictures of Mars and its moons and enabled scientists to draw a complete map of the planet. For the first time the huge Martian volcanoes could be seen. One of them, Mount Olympus, rises to 24 kilometres above the surface!

In 1971 the Russians attempted to make the first soft landings on Mars. Both attempts failed. The first spacecraft crashed. The second Mars lander survived, but its TV signals stopped only 20 seconds after it touched down.

No Trace of Life

It was 1976 before two American Viking spacecraft made the first successful soft landings on Mars. They sent back pictures showing that the surface is covered in rocks. It was found that the Martian sky is pink, instead of blue like Earth's. The temperatures are also lower than on Earth, because Mars is further away from the Sun.

Martian soil: sand dunes and large rocks photographed by Viking 1 and 2

The Vikings scooped up soil from the surface of Mars and studied it to see if any form of life existed. Scientists were disappointed that there was no trace of any life. It is too early to say definitely that there is no life of any kind on Mars. But we do know that there aren't any Martians!

Cold and Unfriendly

Mars is a cold and rather unfriendly world. Even so, it is more like Earth than any of the other planets in the solar system. This is why space scientists have chosen it as the first planet for manned exploration rather than Venus, which is nearer to Earth.

Space Stations

The first rocket to take men to another planet will not travel directly from Earth. It will probably be launched from a space station in orbit round the Earth. It is easier to set out into deep space from a space station than directly from Earth. You do not need such a powerful rocket to take you out of the Earth's gravity.

Both the Russians and Americans have already built space stations. The first space station was launched by the Russians in April 1971. It was called Salyut 1. It was 20 metres long and weighed 19 tonnes.

Special Exercises and Tests

Three cosmonauts travelled up to it in a Soyuz spacecraft. They docked with the space station and then went aboard it. They spent 23 days living and working in it.

While they were on board the cosmonauts did special exercises and tests. Before sending men into space for several weeks, Russia's scientists wanted to know how they would be affected by being weightless for a long time. The cosmonauts had to run on a moving belt, lift weights and do gymnastics. They even had to wear a special kind of spacesuit which made it difficult for them to move. They nicknamed it their penguin outfit.

Tragedy

The mission had gone as planned. Now the cosmonauts undocked their Soyuz capsule and prepared to return to Earth. They re-entered the Earth's atmosphere. The giant parachutes opened and the capsule floated down to the ground.

The recovery team hurried towards it and opened the hatch. They stared in horror. The three cosmonauts were dead. The first trip to a space station had ended in tragedy. An air valve on the Soyuz capsule had started to leak just before re-entry. The cosmonauts had suffocated.

Several other Salyut space stations have been launched during the 1970s. Russian cosmonauts have lived in them for up to three months, carrying out scientific experiments and sending information back to Earth.

Central control panel of Salyut type space station photographed during training

Skylab

The first American space station, called Skylab, was launched in May 1973. It was badly damaged during the launch. The heat shield was torn off. One of the solar wings was ripped away and the other one jammed.

Skylab went into orbit as planned. But the astronauts who should have followed it into space 24 hours later stayed on the ground. It looked as if their mission would have to be called off.

Training model of Skylab's workshop. Shown here is crew quarters section where crew can sleep, eat and conduct experiments

A Major Emergency

Ten days later, however, they took off. The flight to Skylab went well, but then came a major emergency. They were unable to dock their Apollo capsule with Skylab. For four hours they struggled in vain. They decided to make one final attempt, before making an emergency flight back to Earth. At last they succeeded.

Now they set about repairing the damaged space station. First they put up a special sunshade where the heat shield should have been. Then they made a spacewalk and freed the jammed solar wing.

In the Skylab space station astronaut Conrad undergoes a dental examination standing on his head! In the weightlessness of space there is nothing to hold him except the strap round his left leg. Note the floating piece of paper on the right

An artist's impression of how the Skylab space station will be boosted into a higher orbit to prevent it from re-entering Earth's atmosphere

A Great Success

The mission turned out to be a great success. Two more crews followed them aboard Skylab. Altogether the crews spent 171 days in it. They studied the Sun through a special telescope and collected a huge amount of scientific information. 'Skylab worked better broken', said one astronaut, 'than anybody had hoped for if it was perfect.'

Future space stations will not only be used as laboratories. They will be used as workshops where engineers will study the best ways of building and assembling spaceships in orbit. The parts for the spaceships will be carried to the space stations by space shuttles.

Space Shuttles

The Saturn rockets, which took America's astronauts to the Moon, each cost thousands of millions of dollars. But they could only be used once. Space shuttles will have rockets that can be used several times.

The first space shuttle has two main parts – the booster section and the orbiter. Two booster rockets carry the orbiter about 50 kilometres above the Earth. The parts then separate and the boosters parachute into the sea.

The orbiter goes into orbit. It visits the space station, then returns to Earth. Because it has wings like an ordinary aircraft, the orbiter can land on a runway. It can make at least 100 flights.

The space shuttle makes spaceflight much

cheaper. Once larger space stations have been built, it will be easier to travel to and from the Moon. A spacecraft could make regular trips between space stations orbiting the Moon and space stations orbiting the Earth. It could carry minerals that have been mined on the Moon.

The orbiter space shuttle is taken for a test flight on the back of a 747.

45

Drawing of a space shuttle take-off. The orbiter space shuttle is attached to booster rockets which will take it out of Earth's atmosphere

Drawing showing how the space shuttle's external tank will be used in Earth's orbit as the first step of a space platform

Into the Depths of Space

In the very distant future man may travel not only to the planets but out beyond them into the depths of space. A journey to the stars in a present-day spacecraft would take millions of years. The Apollo spacecraft reached a speed of 40 000 k.p.h. on its journey to the Moon. At this speed it would take 280 million years to reach the nearest star. But, in time to come, who knows how fast a starship may be able to travel?

SPACE SHIP

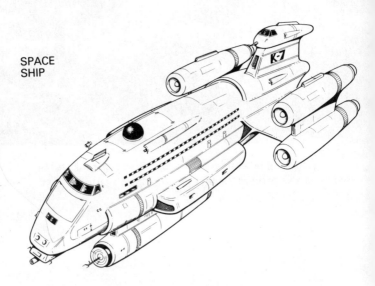